The Christian Home

The Christian Home

By George Weaver
(revised by M. J. Baer)

Reprinted by
Rod and Staff Publishers Inc.
P.O. Box 3, Hwy. 172
Crockett, Kentucky 41413
Telephone: (606) 522-4348

Originally published in 1854 as
THE CHRISTIAN HOUSEHOLD

Copyright 1996
Rod and Staff Publishers Inc.
Crockett, Kentucky 41413

Printed in U.S.A

ISBN 0-7399-0206-7
Catalog no. 2170

6   7   8   9   10   —   16   15   14   13   12   11   10   09   08   07

Table Of Contents

Preface to the Revised Edition

In 1975 this book was condensed by Rod and Staff Publishers into a smaller booklet, also entitled *The Christian Home*. Because of the value of the whole book, a greater effort has been made in this edition to incorporate more of the original work. The need of our day, we believe, warrants a full application of all the pertinent truths that can be acquired on this valuable subject.

This book was originally published in 1854, under the name *The Christian Household*. Since the basic needs of the Christian home are the same today as they were then, we believe that the fathers and mothers of our time will be able to profit greatly from the contents of this writing as they seek to apply Scriptural principles in their homes.

—**M. J. B.**

Preface to the First Edition

This book is designed as a partial answer to the great need of the Christian family. I have for years seen and sorrowed over the absence of Christ in many households. Among the Christian people of every sect there is a sad deficiency of Christian principle and practice at home. The devotion and the love of the Gospel life are alarmingly absent from too many of these sacred places. Thousands of professedly Christian families are unvisited by a song of praise or a voice of prayer, or anything else that distinguishes them from those who scoff at religion. Why is it so? Is it not because, in the Christian race set before us, our doctrine has outrun our conviction and commitment? Have we not preached and practiced more theology than Christian principle and life?

What does doctrine avail if it does not produce life? Doctrine is good, even necessary. It is the seed. But it does not benefit much if it is not accompanied by conviction to put it into practice. The nurturing of the seed from its sowing to its fruit bearing is true religion. It is as necessary to cultivate as to sow. Christians have not sown too much, but have cultivated too little; they have not had too much doctrine, but have had too little true religion.

This book is sent out as a cultivator among the long rows of theological plants. The author is as sensible as anyone to its defects. But he asks the men and women of the world into whose hands it may fall, to read it as it has been written, with a deep and earnest desire for Christian improvement.

We need more books on the home. Home is the heart of the world and the church. If one home is made more Christlike and happy because of this book, it will be well that I have given it to the public.

—**G. S. W.**

Chapter 1

What Is a Christian Home?

Some things are lovely by their very nature. They win our hearts by their inborn beauty, rather than by any effort of their own. In this book we have tried to present a little "art gallery" of such things. These pictures are presented as examples to inspire all who care to look at them. Designed by God, they are true as far as the copyist's hand has proved skillful.

The theme of this effort can be expressed in two of the richest words in human language. The first word describes our divine relationship to God and our human duty to our brother, as well as the blessing that grows out of them. It encompasses the full meaning of moral perfection and virtue. Though it is of earth, this word comes from and points to heaven and is full of that which makes heaven. The word is *Christian*, a common but glorious word.

The second word is one of the most affectionate ones we can use. It carries the heart around the whole circuit of love at one sweep. It includes husband, wife, father, mother, brother, sister, child, and friend, but means more than any one of these words alone. Brimful of tenderness, it includes the whole family cluster. The word is *home*.

Unite these two words, and you have the theme of our book, *the Christian home*. This phrase speaks of tenderness and love coupled with benevolence and duty, made radiant by wisdom from above. Two richer, sweeter words cannot be found, and each is made more expressive by its union with the other.

Consider them a moment. To be a Christian is to possess and cherish the graces of soul and adornments of character that Christ Himself portrayed. The Christian has a heart, filled with active kindness and universal love, that reaches up to God and that embraces all humanity, even his enemies. A real Christian is so wrapped up in his love for God and his desire to please God that he cheerfully obeys the Golden Rule and does not balk at submitting his passions to God's direction.

The person that has been filled with Christian love rises high above the world. He resists his natural passions and selfish desires as he would resist a deadly plague, not allowing them to rule him. He receives the strength from God to overcome evil by prayer. The love that controls him is altogether a godly love, dictated and sustained by God Himself and cherished by a submitted will. This submitted will receives its commands from God and follows the precepts revealed by Christ rather than the desires of the flesh. The Christian has been delivered from the power of sin that once controlled him. As the Bible says, "He is a new creature: old things are passed away; behold, all things are become new" (2 Corinthians 5:17). This is the real meaning of the word *Christian*.

The idea behind the word *home* is hardly less significant. A home is something more than a place to stay, eat, and sleep, where no one may invade without permission. Though all of these factors are included in the home, they fall short of defining the word *home* in its proper and highest sense. A poet once said, "'Tis home where e'er the heart is." Or, perhaps we could say it this way: Where there is no love, there is no home.

Every home is a place, but not every place is a home. Riches and luxury will not turn a house into a home. People may live together in a house, but if love is not present, it is not a home. Only when affection is doing its humble duty, forgiving and sympathizing, is there a home. Home, then, is affection's constant dwelling place.

What, then, is a *Christian home?* It is a place where

the father and mother love each other, their family, and God; where human affection is consecrated by divine love; and where natural love is subdued, chastened, and elevated in Christian goodness.

The Christian home is a place where the Christian graces are both taught and practiced. What could be more reasonable? Piety should be evident at home, in the place where the heart lives, where young souls come into being. Here children are taught lessons they will never forget, and here the foundation of the Christian church is laid. Is it unreasonable to expect that Christianity should be cultivated around the home table? Should not godliness be the daily guest in every home? Where is divine instruction more in order than in our homes? Dwelling places cannot be homes without the expression of living truth.

No home is without its trials. Can any other power sustain us through the days and weeks of prolonged suffering like the consciousness of the presence of a loving heavenly Father who watches over His own? When bodily strength fails, when the tongue falters and all is finally over, those who are left must face the cold, desolate grave that waits to receive the body of their loved one. A vacant seat, keepsakes, and garments left behind do little to relieve the aching void. Is there any balm for such an hour of trial? Yes, if Christ is there. His Word tells us that those who die in the Lord will be with Him forever. Through this we learn the blessedness that sometimes sorrow alone can yield, the submission it calls for, the resignation and trust it teaches, and the faith it encourages. Through Christ a family can rise up calm and strengthened, still mourning but not without hope.

No home can well do without the divine power of a holy God, for all homes are exposed to the power of the wicked one. Any responsible parent would tremble at the thought of raising a child without the sustaining aid of the divine Comforter. What parent who does not pray constantly for the spiritual welfare of his children can sleep peacefully or awake joyfully? No mature person can rest a moment if he does not know the refreshing and cheerful gift of Christian faith and peace. No home without a living faith is safe, because no home without God is strong.

Trials of various natures visit every home—business problems, vexations and disappointments, misdemeanors, errors, differences of opinion, and days of loneliness and bitter reflection. If the inhabitants of the home have not cultivated the spiritual strength that sustains in times of trouble, the distresses will seem insurmountable. This is where the home with a firm confidence in an almighty God finds its peace and rest. There will be a balance, a quiet resting place for troubled souls, and a balm for the holy affections.

Sin in all its forms will always threaten the home. Without our constant vigilance, sin can grow and spread right in the heart of a home. Homes that neglect their spiritual welfare become wretched places in which to live. We must be careful that none of our homes accept this wretchedness as normal.

A Christian home must be built according to the pattern given us in the Holy Word. Prayer and intercession, accompanied by a living example of holiness, must be practiced constantly. Those who do this will enjoy the peace of God in their homes, but it will come only at the summons of intercessory prayer and fasting, and will tarry only at the constant request of the faithful ones.

In recommending piety at home, Paul wrote, "But if any widow have children or nephews, let them learn first to shew piety at home, and to requite their parents: for that is good and acceptable before God" (1 Timothy 5:4). If we note that these words are addressed to the young, we will better understand what Paul meant by the instruction. Piety is usually regarded as a devoted spirit of submission to God. But the word means more than this. It formerly meant all that a child should feel and do to fulfill his duty to his parents. This concept of piety combined reverence, gratitude, and love. Without doubt, this is the apostle's meaning. He as much as said, Let them learn to show respect, gratitude, and love for such is really the service due a parent from a child. Whether parents or children who have come to the age of accountability, we all bear the same relation to God.

Thus a complete self-consecration and reverence toward God should temper our natural love and disposition. If we say we love God and do not perform the outward acts of love, we deceive ourselves; our love is not true (see 1 John 2:9–11). It is only a momentary passion or sudden impulse, for love makes good all its professions; it is more tender in action than it can possibly be in word. So if we say we have reverence and love for God but do not perform the appropriate actions of respect, praise, and devotion, we deceive ourselves.

How do we show piety in the home? The ways are numerous, but we will mention a few.

1. Respect the Name of God. The Name of God should never be spoken lightly or thoughtlessly, either in jest or in passion. It should never be used profanely, but with deep respect, as a Name too sacred, too great, and too dear to awaken feelings other than holiness, respect, and gratitude. This great Name, when spoken, should inspire love for the great Being who bears it and should always remind us of our Father in heaven.

2. Respect the Word of God. God's Word should never be spoken of irreverently or disparagingly. Portions should be made a daily study so that its wisdom and treasures may become each family member's personal possession.

There is a divine power in the Word that elevates and transforms the soul that reads it attentively and with understanding. The Psalms, the Proverbs, the prophecies, and the writings of Moses are rich with inspiring influences for good. The instructions of Christ and His apostles are the highest forms of moral teachings ever given to man. The Word of God is the only chart of life, the only guide to blessedness, and the only sure light of life. How important that it should be treasured in the home. Where the grand law of Christ is made the law of the home, what a picture of heaven is presented on earth!

3. Respect good reading material. Books that diffuse piety and practical goodness; devotional works designed to comfort, strengthen, and encourage; and works that explain and illustrate divine truths, clarify the doctrines of the Gospel, strengthen faith, and brighten hopes should be found in every Christian home. Biographies of good men and women who were outstanding for their piety and service should be read at home for both benefit and enjoyment. Great is the power of good books to mold a strong and noble character, and great is the pleasure of reading and understanding their glorious lessons. Much may be gathered into the treasure house of home by reading about our godly forefathers and the martyrs of our faith. These then become guardians of our homes and breathe their virtues into our own souls.

4. Keep your family conversation in good order. Conversation upon moral and religious subjects; upon service, home, and heaven; and upon teachings of the Bible should be carried on freely at home, and all should engage in it. Such conversation is exceptionally useful. It cultivates the power of expression, elevates the mind, and leaves the family with fond memories of home.

5. Sing the songs of Zion together. Sacred music does much to elevate the home. Hymns of praise and devotion have a subduing and chastening influence, and they should be sung often in the home. They are of special assistance in preparing for a meaningful devotional life. Such singing will awaken the tender feelings that belong in every home.

6. Take time for family worship. Families should have devotional exercises from the Bible every day. Such inspiration will help us much in our worship to our Lord.

7. Pray together. Nothing breathes such tender harmonies through the home as devout and earnest prayer. In every family the voice of prayer should often be heard. True prayer always inspires a resolution to good and appeals to our nobler nature. Hence the more that devotional feelings are cultivated in a family, the more virtuous the family will be.

8. Be kind. Kindness should be the crowning virtue of every Christian home. Come what may, every member of the home should be taught to practice kindness in word, look, and action. Kindness should be understood as the home's inviolable law and should reign above all, even when differences of opinion arise and interests seem to clash.

It is the presence or absence of the Spirit of divine love that makes a home godly or otherwise. By strictly attending to the above principles, we will maintain a godly home. Such homes preach righteousness to the communities where they are found—a living righteousness imbued with power from God. In them are nursed the messengers of peace, the oracles of wisdom, and the conservators of virtue and true godliness. They constitute a power far greater than a thousand blazing cannons. Would you be a blessing to the world? Would you live for Christ and His cause? Establish for yourself a Christian home.

Study Questions

Questions are included at the end of each chapter for class discussion. However, we encourage discussion leaders to add practical questions pertinent to the age and experience of the class, and to take time to discuss questions from the class.

Do not depend just on this book for answers, but reach into your own experience and the teaching of the Bible to go beyond the scope of this book. In order to be useful, any discussion of the Christian home needs to be both practical and encouraging.

1. Why are the words *Christian* and *home* so all-encompassing when combined?

2. Why is it important that all who are part of a Christian home have their wills submitted to God?

3. Why is truth a significant pillar for the Christian home?

4. Why is a living faith necessary in a Christian home?

5. Explain why sin is out of place in the Christian home.

6. What is piety?

7. Discuss some practical ways that piety is expressed in the Christian home.

Wives,
submit yourselves unto your own
husbands, as unto the Lord.

Husbands,
love your wives, even as Christ also
loved the church, and gave himself
for it.

For this cause
shall a man leave his father and mother,
and shall be joined unto his wife,
and they two shall be one flesh.

—Ephesians 5:22, 25, 31

Chapter 2

The Christian Husband

When man was created, his Maker declared that it was not good for him to be alone; therefore He worked out His divine plan for the Christian home (see Genesis 2:18–24). God placed the first man and woman in a blessed state of perfection. This first human pair fell into sin, and their fall caused an abrupt change in man's state. But God in His divine foreknowledge granted them probationary grace. Even though they were cursed because of sin, God sent them out of the garden to propagate the race from which, in the fullness of time, the divine Redeemer would come.

If the marriage union were understood as God intended it, today's careless immorality could not exist.

The first marriage was an act of God, as are all marriages. God alone is the maker of marriages. Without God's blessing, there is no truly spiritually satisfying marriage. He does allow for marriage outside His divine economy, but the fulfillment of His plan for the home calls for Christian marriage and godly living.

Marriage is a divine institution. God presided at the first marriage and still performs the solemn rite of indissoluble union for both the Christian and the non-Christian. He more than sanctioned marriage—He ordained it and instituted its relations. He wove the cord of love that binds two willing hearts into one. In God's plan, marriage is a Christian institution. It has its origin and sanction in the God who instituted it, and should always be thus regarded.

Since God is love (1 John 4:8), it is only natural that God would establish a union that mirrors His own loving nature in His creation. The very fact of marriage shows that God designed the fountain of love in this world and desired to keep it flowing forever. In its proper sphere, marriage is the garden of all affections and the nursery of all sanctified love. Christian marriage, then, should be considered a precept of divine wisdom, which when obeyed will make marriage all that God intended it to be.

Every man who marries should be a Christian and regard all his duties as responses to a sacred trust that can be carried out only under the guidance and direction of a holy God. When, at his marriage, he takes the confiding hand of his companion, a man ought to understand the holy ideal of fulfilling what God intended in His initial purposes for Christian marriage. His vows should be a complete consecration to life's most sacred duties.

Too many have viewed marriage as a mere civil compact or as a social contract for earthly convenience or sordid pleasure and have debased it by brutal tyranny and lust. Such living is only licensed licentiousness—a brutal trampling upon the divine institution of marriage. The common idea of marriage is far too low and sordid. Few appreciate the excellence of this institution or its highest object; nor can they, unless they understand fully the holy principle that God intended for a Christian home.

No ungodly man can make a full and perfect husband. He can neither respond to all the needs of his wife's soul nor encourage her best ambitions. He cannot reciprocate her holiest love. A man's sweetest and most cherished companionship is the answer to his wife's spiritual yearnings, but an ungodly man cannot provide such companionship. If his wife yearns for it, she cannot find it in him. She must yearn on through life, having a companion only for her lower nature, while her higher nature remains unfulfilled. Many sorrows are associated with such an unsatisfying union. Only Christ can give the answer to such an unsatisfactory state.

Such unholy situations should warn us about the extreme care an individual must take in choosing a life companion. Courtship should not be entered without true spiritual consecration and guidance, because the consequences are too crucial and binding. Even though a worldly husband be ever so kind, he sadly lacks an understanding of the deep spiritual needs of a truly healthy marriage. This kind of marriage, although binding for life, seldom achieves that for which it was instituted.

Herein lies one of the great retributions for failure in duty; it is God's reproof for violating His great law for marriage. Marriage is both an inner and an outer union. Within the spirit lie the secret springs of joy and blessedness. Hence the husband who fails to regard marriage in such a light cannot attain even a proper affection for his wife. To feed and clothe her and meet her physical needs is not to be her companion in the highest sense of the term. True companionship lies in answering the call of a woman's spirit, a call whose nature is spiritual and that pertains to the immortal woman. These calls originate in the soul, and the husband who does not meet them is not a true husband. He is not the companion of his wife's soul and does not love her as he ought.

In our society, the man is responsible to propose marriage. The woman can accept or reject the proposal. The promises a man makes are summed up in this one, that he will nurture her whole nature—that he will clothe, protect, and adorn her soul as well as her body. If a man loves his wife as he ought, with a noble, dignified, and

Christian affection, he will recognize these duties and cheerfully and faithfully perform them. As it was he who asked for the companionship and voluntarily led the way to it, so he will assume the lead in every Christian duty and provide the depth for their spiritual relationship.

In all these duties, he is to maintain the lead, asking his wife to assist him with her advice, encouragement, and affection. He has constituted himself an example for her, a pioneer in their journey of life, spiritually as well as temporally. He has placed himself at the head, saying to his wife, "By my side and under the shadow and safety of my good right arm shalt thou walk."

But what are his spiritual duties to his wife? They are the cultivation and happiness of her mind and the development and culture of her soul's powers and capacities. His reason for taking her was to enjoy a companionship that would bless them both.

The motivation for this sacred union can be properly realized only if both persons desire first the spiritual enhancement of themselves and all they encounter. In all things they must be one, especially in united prayer. For the blessings of heaven to fall upon them, their spirits must become one as they kneel at the throne of grace, together holding daily communion with God.

The duties of a Christian husband include the following:

1. He must feed with his wife on the Holy Word.

Here we find Moses, Isaiah, and Paul. What can inspire the intellect more than the example of such men? And what can quicken an ascending soul better than the Holy Spirit, who breathes and glows like a divine glory through their lives?

If a husband wants to develop the best and most blessed state for his home life, he will find it at the shrine of devotion. It will quicken his soul, sanctify his life, and sweeten every area of his marriage. Because a man marries his wife, both soul and body, he must nourish both. The more he cherishes her soul, the less she will desire the lesser and mundane things of life. Everybody with industry, temperance, and economy can find enough time and means for all the religious reading that life requires.

2. He must take his family to public worship. Public worship is a necessity for a balanced spiritual home. Husband and wife should attend together so that both are spiritually refreshed. A discerning husband will seek a church that provides grace to the home as both he and his wife are fed with heavenly manna in the weekly meetings. Church attendance should be neglected no more than the daily meals or everyday labor of life. The responsible husband will desire this more than worldly luxuries and riches.

3. He must establish regular family worship. Family worship is one of the most powerful means of Christian enrichment available for the Christian family. The influence of family worship goes far beyond the walls of the home, and no husband should neglect this private and personal means of improvement. A man may lead out in family devotions despite his past life, no matter how great a sinner he may have been or how unworthy he may feel before God. He will not find it difficult to read a daily Scripture lesson, lead a hymn of praise, and offer a fervent prayer to God. This experience will grow better each time it is exercised and will become a blessing each evening or morning. By attending to these duties, the husband will lead his family closer to the true Lord of his household and will attain to the full stature of a Christian husband. Spiritual growth should be the constant aim of every Christian's life, and especially of the Christian husband.

Christian progress should be the goal of every Christian couple. Only by heeding its inspiring spirit and by demonstrating its glorious meaning can a husband prove that he fully obeys the apostolic injunction, "Husbands, love your wives."

Study Questions

1. How does God view non-Christian marriage?

2. Which of God's attributes is especially reflected in a Christian marriage? How is it manifested?

3. What was God's initial intent for establishing marriage?

4. What spiritual enhancement is found only in a Christian union?

5. Who bears the greatest responsibility for meeting the spiritual needs of the Christian home?

6. Discuss the practical outworking of the husband's duties in the Christian home.

7. How can the Christian husband establish and maintain his leadership role without demeaning or belittling his wife's role?

8. What are some practical ways in which the Christian husband can obey the Bible command to love his wife?

Blessed is every one that feareth the LORD; that walketh in his ways.
For thou shalt eat the labour of thine hands:

Happy shalt thou be,
and it shall be well with thee.

Thy wife shall be as a fruitful vine by the sides of thine house:
thy children like olive plants round about thy table.

Behold, that thus shall the man be blessed that feareth the LORD.

—Psalm 128:1–4

Chapter 3

The Christian Wife

God completed His universe by creating woman. When she first came from the divine hand, untouched by sin and unmarred by error, woman was as perfect an expression of the divine image as could be created in flesh.

But a woman deluded by ignorance and seduced by sin is quite another creature. She has sadly defaced and scarred the soul that God gave her. She has become a partner with man in weakness, error, and guilt, and now, by nature, she fails to see herself as she ought, to fill her proper sphere, to do her legitimate work, or to feel her holy responsibilities.

But Christianity has a mission for her. If she answers

its call to duty, she can embody its ideal of beauty and best express its spiritual excellence.

Woman is properly regarded as the love element of humanity. She is love, while man is power; that is, her strength is love, while his is power. She is love and thought; he is power and thought. In strength of intellect the two are equal. In hard thought, in correct observation, in close analysis they stand together.

Yet though equal here, there is a difference. Woman is quicker, more understanding, and intuitive; man is more plodding, analytical, and argumentative. But in the realm of love she wears the crown; in the realm of power he does. This difference adapts each to the other and, when they are united, makes each stronger and more efficient.

Christianity is consecrated love, or love in its highest, perfect, heavenly form. Hence it is exceptionally adapted to woman's nature. Woman is in her highest estate when she becomes a Christian. Her soul is now flooded with divine intuition and direction. Her heart, acting in its highest capacity, harmonizes with Christianity's great principles.

Christ embodied pure affection. His precepts were the natural speech of celestial tenderness; His life was a picture of perfect love. Thus His teachings have always found a ready response in the Christian woman's heart. She was His last friend at the cross and His first at the sepulcher. He appeared to her first after the resurrection. The first person commissioned to herald tidings of that great event, the resurrection, was a woman.

Woman outside Christianity has always been degraded. Because love is timid and yielding, she has usually shrunk from the contest of power with her companion;[1] and because power is exacting and arbitrary, he has held the rein fast and has too often made his companion a slave. Christianity breaks this chain and grants woman full companionship with man in their mutual life in Christ.

Woman, as a wife, is in her truest and most beautiful position. Here she occupies a natural field that will delight her as none other can; one to which her nature will always tend and in which her powers will develop more beautifully and harmoniously than elsewhere. She aspires to this because she has invited here her strongest affection. This is the great harvest field of her love, and because it opens to her the duties of the most tender relations of life, it is here she appears in her noblest aspect. Home, the lone earthly type of heaven, is woman's domain. In it she presides with a grace all her own, with

---

[1]

This is not as true as it was in the days it was written. Since the advent of the women's liberation movement, some women see men more as rivals than as companions. —EDITOR

singular dignity and propriety. However much woman may exert her influence in the world, it is in her home that she finds her richest enjoyments and extends her most potent control. She will find her greatest satisfaction in carrying out her God-given responsibilities in her home. She can never do more than in her rightful place in her home. Here her strength will build pyramids, and she will erect monuments of love and loyalty. Here she will yield her greatest influence and extend her mightiest power.

A woman's influence at home is not narrow. The words she speaks and the deeds she does at home will have their effect throughout the church and even at the judgment bar of God.

How can a woman who is not a Christian and who therefore has not determined to live a Christian life become a wife? In marrying a man, she takes within her embrace the human being she loves more than any other. Her influence upon him is more potent and penetrating than any other earthly influence in his life. To her he opens his heart, wherein she assumes her rightful place. He shares his confidences with her, which she accepts with that gratitude that makes her thereafter their keeper.

A woman's character will be mirrored in her husband's, whether bright or dark, pure or impure. The moment they are united, their characters begin to blend like the mingling waters of two streams that meet. The currents which before were two now merge to become one. There *are* exceptions, but the general rule is that a wife exerts a potent influence over her husband and the complexion of that influence is the same in his character as in hers. If good in her, it will be good in him; if bad in her, it will be bad in him. If Christian in her, it will be a Christian influence on him; if worldly in her, she will be a worldly pressure on him.

This being a solemn fact, I ask again, how can a woman truly become a wife with no Christian principles, with no baptism of her spirit at the cleansing fountain? If she appreciates the solemn issues of the office she is to fill, if she comprehends anything of the responsibility she is about to assume, she will not try it.

People are too apt to look indifferently on their everyday obligations and to regard the duties of a seemingly narrow sphere as less important than those of a wider one. This is a fatal error; life is made up of little things. If a small thing is well done, we cannot tell how great it may grow. Oaks, rivers, and kingdoms are all small at the beginning. Is it a small thing for one human soul to mold another into the life of Christ? Is it a small thing for one soul to lead another to a virtuous life? Virtue is cumulative to the responsive soul. Like a tree, it spreads its seeds, and other trees result. If a wife plants a virtue in her husband's heart, he gives it to his neighbors and they to theirs. He gives it to his children, and they pass it on to theirs.

Thus virtue spreads outward and upward to infinity. The wife who helps her husband helps build the kingdom of heaven and adorns many souls with robes of white, which they will wear throughout eternity. Little things are therefore not small things. There are no small things in human life; they all have infinite relations.

Therefore no wife is a nonentity. She must affect her husband. As a consecrated unit, they cannot act separately. The wife's influence, then, is perpetual and powerful, whether or not she will have it so. A husband cannot escape it. Into his mind she pours a constant stream of influence, good or bad; it is for her to say which.

Wives are too apt to think they stand on neutral ground while their husbands do as they please. This is not true. A wife fills a large place in her husband's soul. It is her business to be sure that her influence helps him do what is right.

She may not always succeed in doing all she would for him, but she must always try. If she works in wisdom and love, she will do him some good. By uniting with him, she sets the current of his life, and it is now her business to see, as far as she can, that it flows always in the right direction. She is a wife and will exert an influence. The question is How shall she be a Christian wife unto her husband?

First of all, she must be a Christian woman. In true repentance she must lay her own carnal nature on the altar of God and ask Him to make her a daughter of His. She must enshrine Christ in her heart, and she must love and cherish His principles. She must be inwardly conformed to the right, in love with that which is morally beautiful and true. If these principles are not alive in her heart, she will never succeed in exerting a Christian influence on her husband. She cannot pass on to him what she herself does not possess. Her mightiest influence over him must come from her own heart.

Her first work, therefore, is to see to her own heart. By fervently devoting and submitting her spirit to the blessed Saviour, she will open a door of communion with God and consecrate herself to the duties of His devout and obedient children. Thus prepared, she will have a hallowed influence, and the natural, everyday outworking of her spirit will tend to Christianize her home.

Every Christian duty harmonizes with a pious woman's heart, and every Christian principle is in unison with the inmost feelings of the godly wife. The more she loves God, the more she loves her husband. She devotes herself to her husband's good. She consecrates her heart to a love for her husband that corresponds to the love that the Christian feels for all. She employs her hand in ministering to the wants of her household, while through Christ she devotes her hand to the needy of all families.

The Christian woman's spiritual nature will show forth its excellence in her life. She will show Christian love and duty to her husband, thus allowing her spirit to soften and sweeten his stern nature and refine the coarseness of his outward life so that her home becomes the dwelling place of refinement and affection.

She should make use of all godly means to bring about the Christian improvement of her family. A Christian heart and life are not inherited, nor are they unbought gifts. They are only attained by giving up self-will to God in true repentance. The Christian woman cannot force her husband or children to do this, but she can do much to influence them in the right direction. Her own godly example will draw their minds heavenward. Her submission to God's plan in her own life will help them to submit their spirits to Him.

There are some things that should be part of every Christian family's experience. The first is church attendance. Few things are more conducive to ordering a household well. Regular church attendance affords a constant and uniform Sunday observance, which of itself is beneficial and promotes every Christian virtue.

When a Christian family returns home from a church service, its members' hearts should be attuned to each other, as well as to the truth and to the principles of Gospel love and peace. Then everything in their home will reflect the harmony in their hearts. The thoughts they have heard and the feelings they have enjoyed afford topics for discussion. Thus they renew the sanctuary service and further its holy themes. A good sermon, heard and forgotten, does little good. Even a poorly presented one, heard, remembered, conversed about, and improved upon, may do great good.

These home exercises are highly profitable but greatly neglected in most families. Engaging in them will depend in no small degree upon the wife, who is often the most influential member of the household at home. If she faithfully attends public worship and uses her best influence over her household to secure their attendance with her, and then follows up the service with the proper supplement of home conversation, she exerts upon her family a Christian influence that cannot well be calculated. In this way every wife may be of great service in teaching her family Christian principles.

Another means of effecting Christian improvement in the home is religious reading, instruction, and devotion. Though family devotions are primarily under the husband's authority, in homes where the husband does not lead out, the wife must endeavor to fill this gap in her children's lives, perhaps by reading them Bible stories and teaching them Christian songs, and certainly by giving godly training and example. And where the husband does assume his proper leadership in this area, the wife should assist and cooperate with him. Nothing pleases a Christian husband more than the knowledge that his wife is devoted to his family's spiritual good.

A woman may do much to Christianize her home. She may gently check the tendencies to error, stay the progress of corrupt thoughts, curb the use of improper and coarse language, restrain the vehemence of passion, and introduce into every department an elevating tendency. This is the spiritual office of a wife.

She should be an evangel of peace and virtue to her husband. To succeed in this, she must be zealous and earnest; she must not become weary in well doing. This requires a patient, persevering, cheerful devotion to her divine Lord. Because she might not feel full satisfaction in her labors every day, she must learn to labor and to wait. Then she will reap in due season (see Galatians 6:9).

These spiritual duties do not in any way interfere with a wife's household duties. To be a Christian, a woman must be faithful in all these. Her Christian feelings and philosophy will lend purpose and dignity to all her daily labors. They will teach her to make every labor of life, every little duty, minister to the spiritual benefit of herself and her family. Every domestic service will become a shrine upon which some beautiful and acceptable sacrifice can be offered.

If all wives were Christian, fewer husbands would go astray. A Christian wife is man's greatest, holiest blessing. Would that there were more Christian wives! The world needs them, and some men deserve them. No words can express the blessedness of their mission.

Study Questions

1. In what way are the man and the woman equal?

2. What are some differences between man and woman that complement each other in the Christian home?

3. Why and how is a Christian wife's good influence on her home dependent on her personal relationship with God?

4. In what ways does a Christian wife exert her greatest influence?

5. Why do the little, everyday things in the life of the Christian wife tend to grow to great importance?

6. Explain the extent of the Christian wife's influence over her husband and her children.

7. Discussing sermons and Sunday school lessons with her husband and her children will enhance the Christian woman's influence on her family. In what ways?

8. List some areas of direct influence that the wife and mother has on her family.

9. What are some practical ways in which a Christian wife can obey the Bible command to reverence her husband?

Who can find a virtuous woman?
for her price is far above rubies.

The heart of her husband doth safely trust in her,
so that he shall have no need of spoil.

She will do him good and not evil
all the days of her life.

—Proverbs 31:10–12

Chapter 4

The Christian Father

The father–child relationship is a mysterious one. Many hold it, but few appreciate it. Fathers live in every neighborhood, but how many fathers comprehend the dignity of fatherhood? God is a Father. He is the first, the perfect Father of all, the fountainhead of fatherhood. All fathers have grown out of Him; all parent power has its origin in Him. All humanity has budded and blossomed in the ground of His paternity.

Do fathers revere the source of their parentage? It is irreverent to become a father without a prayer to the Giver of all paternity.

Father is a title of tenderness, but one that brings serious responsibilities. It was not blessing enough that

God created man in His own image, but He conferred upon him the power to engender other men in His image. The father gives himself to his child; he remakes himself; he molds his character into his child's. Usually a brutal father begets a brutal child, whereas a high-souled father imparts nobility to his child.

How fearful a thing, then, it is to be a father! The evil influence of his faults, imperfections, weaknesses, impulses, passions, ruling loves, and lusts stand daily before the child. In this way they may pass as an inheritance from generation to generation unless checked by the power of God Himself in the life of the child.

On the other hand, how beautiful a thing it may be to be a father! His strong affections and virtues, his noble powers and generous spirit, his goodness and large-heartedness are also an influence that will strike root in the soil of the new soul and go down to succeeding generations as a rich paternal inheritance. To this influence for good, no man can set any bounds.

How great a thing it is to be a father! What powerful results may follow in the line of a father's family! Many an unknown father has made the nations shake with his son's or daughter's name. Tremendous effects for good or bad often follow fathers of modest bearing. The stream that flows from every sire could well be mighty. Truly, it is a great, a fearful, and a beautiful thing to be a father.

To be a Christian father, then, in the fullest and

strongest sense, to impart the most powerful Christian influence to a child and impress upon his nature the richest inheritance of good, a man must begin the work of Christianizing his own soul long before he becomes a father. He cannot pass on an inheritance till he has something to give; he cannot impart a good that is not in him; he cannot confer a force that he does not possess. The greater the Christian force a man has in him, the greater the abundance of right over wrong, of good over evil, of Christ over Belial, in his own character the greater will be the inheritance of good he will confer upon his child.

A man cannot turn himself into a Christian. He must kneel at the foot of the cross in repentance and submission and allow God to do His transforming work in him. Thus may Christianity be wrought into a man's soul. Not only its doctrines, but also its moral force and its Spirit may ingrain itself into his spirit, may permeate his mental being and invigorate his nobler nature so that his tendency is heavenward. Perfection cannot be accomplished in a day, a week, or even a year, but the silent workings of the Holy Spirit in his life will do much for him. Justification is an instantaneous work of Christ. Sanctification is a progressive work and requires time proportional to its magnitude.

More than a lifetime would be needed to learn everything. A heart cannot grow to its warmest love, or a soul to its greatest moral vigor, in less time. But the man that gives his heart and soul to God will be a man with a Christian character. He might not be as richly endowed with Christian good as he desires to be before he assumes the responsibilities of paternity, but he can be a Christian and in solemn and earnest sanctification of his soul impart a rich moral inheritance to his offspring by the example of godliness and holiness that he leaves in his everyday life.

The idea of inheritance is immensely important, yet the world seems scarcely to think of it as it relates to human fathers. Plants can be pruned to improve their qualities, but some deem it intolerant to talk of improving human parentage. But whether we accept it or not, inheritance and the possibility for improvement are solemn realities that lie at the very bottom of human existence. God's law is that the parent is the root of the offspring; that the child grows out of the father; and this law can never be annulled. He who is wise will consider the consequences of such a law. "Do men gather grapes of thorns, or figs of thistles?" (Matthew 7:16).

Paternity is an assumed relationship; it is not a fatal necessity laid upon us. In assuming it voluntarily, a man assumes its responsibilities. He tacitly models his ideas of fatherhood according to the highest lights of his age and society. In every culture the highest type of good is in Christ, and so the best father is a Christian father.

By the example of his life, a father effectually imparts himself to his children while they are still young.

The young child's ingrained kindredness with the father makes it natural for the father's example to impress itself upon the child's mind with a peculiar force. The father's authority makes his example still more impressive; then his love fixes his every act upon his child's mind as a righteous one.

The father is the pattern. His law is both wisdom and authority. His words are the true and great words, and the child repeats them as the utterances of an oracle. Whether they are profane or devout, brutal or spiritual, coarse or refined, true or false, the child loves to repeat them over and over again. A son loves to do what he sees his father do and be what his father is. He has no higher ambition than to repeat his father; he knows nothing greater or more desirable.

A child is like a parrot; he loves to repeat. But the child does not mimic just for sport. Mimicry is his business. What he sees done he must do, or at least try to do. The whole effort and labor of childhood is one of imitation. Animals have instincts that guide them to their proper life, but children learn by imitation. This makes it of utmost importance for Christian parents, and especially the Christian father, to be a good example for the child to follow.

The child looks to his parent more naturally than to anyone else for his example. The parent sets the copy; the child writes or scrawls after it. It is thus by the constant and powerful force of example that the father remolds his character in that of his child. His character colors, as it were, his offspring's soul.

The child is a camera before which the father sits to photograph himself on the film of his young. His real character is the one he gives to the child; he cannot cheat him with a pretended character. If the father is a Christian, he will give a Christian coloring to his child; if he is an infidel or a sensualist or a worldling, he will thus impress his child. This is the general and natural result of the paternal pattern. It is always so, save when the paternal example is checked or wholly stayed by other influences. It is natural that the child become a new edition of the father. Herein lies the glory of paternity as well as its greatest challenge.

The father's business and duty is to be a true father, to set a right example before his child, to write him a good life-copy. A father is not compelled to swear, lie, cheat, or steal; to be coarse, vulgar, or irreverent; to desecrate the Lord's Day, the law, or the peace; to be ungenerous, unkind, or unchristian. On the contrary, he has a moral obligation to be the reverse of all these. And this is where a father's solemn moral obligations press upon us.

He has brought into being spirits of an immortal mold, kindred with himself. They may be the forefathers of countless human beings, and upon the characters of these offspring the father is daily impressing his own moral likeness. Think of the tremendous potential for good or evil in this process. The godly father's spiritual fortitude, vision, and guidance may influence a dozen generations to seek their God! On the other hand, the ungodly father's faults, vices, weaknesses, and immoral impulses are also mingling in his children's characters, to mar and make miserable their lives. Even his corrupt thoughts and vicious actions embody themselves in his descendants' spirits and lives. Where will they end? Who can stop the deadly vapor that a father's bad example can engender in his children?

It is true that children sometimes turn out better than their fathers, but sometimes they turn out worse. The father's very badness can disgust the child and make him hate his father's vices and love the virtues that they oppose. But these are exceptions. The rule is that the father's example is imitated by the child. And this rule ought to come home to the hearts of all fathers and touch them with an earnest realization of their paternal responsibility.

A Christian father is morally bound to set a Christian example before his child. When a man assumes the paternal relation, he assumes the sponsorship of an immortal being. He has no moral right to become a father till he has determined to show his child a practical, personal illustration of a true life.

As to specifically what a Christian example is, there need be no discussion. Men differ about Christian doctrines, but about a Christian life they all agree. Men subscribe to different creeds and call them Christian, but all true Christians conform to one spirit and abide by one internal law. Men profess to deny Christianity, but they cannot deny a Christian life. There is but one opinion of a Christian life. To be Christian is to be honest, industrious, and kind; to revere God and love our fellow men; to subdue the lower nature and elevate the spiritual nature; to cherish Christ as our Teacher, Saviour, and Lord; and to entreat wicked men.

A father should live a true life before his children. His offices may be summed up as follows: He is a ruler, a teacher, a protector, and a provider. We will look at each of these in turn.

1. The father has authority over his children. He is, by virtue of his relationship, their governor. He cannot be a Christian father unless he sustains a Christian authority over his children. A family without law is not a Christian family; a father without authority is not a Christian father; children without obedience are not worthy of being in a Christian home.

Obedience to and reverence for proper authority is one of the basic tenets of Christianity, and this should be the primary idea of the family. Bedlam at home is death to home happiness and usefulness. A father should rule with the sceptre of righteous authority.

The rod has a Scriptural use. Better to use the rod wisely than to have bedlam at home. A tempered government is better than no government, even though uncontrolled tyranny is evil and wrong. Solomon said, "Foolishness is bound in the heart of a child; but the rod of correction shall drive it far from him" (Proverbs 22:15). Children are born with a fallen nature and need to be trained to do what is right. They will not do it of their own volition. A Christian father will ensure that his child receives the chastening that he needs. "He that spareth his rod hateth his son: but he that loveth him chasteneth him betimes" (Proverbs 13:24).

The surest way to spoil a child is to let him go ungoverned, to teach him no ideas of obedience, but let his impulses be his master. Moral character rests in obedience. Virtue is another name for obedience. Hence, a child cannot develop firm, reliable moral character till his soul is trained to obey actively and practically an authority that he acknowledges as just.

The goal of authority is to subdue and mold a child's spirit by teaching him obedience to the right. A calm, evenhanded system of kind and gentle discipline, in which the persuasive power of love, directed by wisdom, appears as the chief element, will in most cases secure a steady and happy obedience.

But even in this mild and persuasive course, a strong and steady firmness must rule the ruler. There is no authority in a wavering mind, and none in a weak and volatile purpose. More parents ruin their authority by inconsistency than by any other means. They do not govern themselves. No strong authority of principle rules over them. If they cannot govern themselves, how can they govern their children? The Christian father's first duty is to govern himself, and only then does he possess the power by which he may govern others.

By being first governed by Christian principles himself, a father may mold his children by judiciously applying these principles every day in his family. Divine love—steady, high, moral love—is the governing Christian principle. Natural love, though necessary, is not enough. Natural love must first be sanctified with Christian principle and consecrated by morality before it possesses any authority. When the Christian father rules his family with divine love, his children will grow up around him to spread blessings in his pathway and pronounce benedictions on his head. Generation after generation will honor him, and the Redeemer's kingdom will grow brighter and wider by his authority.

2. The father is his children's natural teacher. They look to him as the foundation of wisdom. The child's first impression of his father is that in him resides all power and knowledge. This attitude on the part of the child invests the Christian father with the authority to be the spiritual tutor of his children. He is their natural priest; he leads their family worship, preaches their sermons, expounds their views, and points out their road to virtue, happiness, and heaven.

Christian fathers who fancy they need not instruct their children in religious knowledge, but let them grow up and get their religious principles as best they can, commit a fatal error. Better to neglect all other instruction!

Who will tell them the wisdom of Christ? Who will instruct them in the Christian doctrines, principles, duties, and joys? It is the Christian father's duty to teach his children Christian truths and principles. If he fails in this, others will teach them heathen error. If the father does not occupy their minds with Christ and His principles, others may occupy them with Belial and his heresies. It is the worst possible exposure to leave children's minds untaught in religion.

A Christian father should teach his children to believe what he believes. He should teach his children to regard as sacred what he considers sacred. And he should teach his children to worship the God he worships. He should indoctrinate them with his theology, and ingrain them with his religion. He should not expect his children to believe any differently than he does.

Every day he should give them lessons. He should teach them of God's paternal care. He should teach them from the living witness of nature and providence that they have a Father in heaven who is too wise to err and too good to do wrong, whom they ought to love with all their heart and obey with all their will. He should teach them the principles of God's moral government as developed in the Gospel of Christ; teach them of Christ, His glorious life of divine goodness, and all that pertains to their spiritual life and final destiny. Thus, by helping them to submit their will to God's will, he will gradually and surely open within them the spiritual flower whose fruit is eternal life, and thus they will step into the Redeemer's vineyard when He calls them to serve Him.

3. The father is the child's natural protector. A child is weak and needs a protector morally as well as physically. The father is that protector. It is especially the Christian father's office to guard his child against the moral and religious evils to which the child is exposed.

Look at the world and see the numerous weeds of error and wickedness! Even the religious field abounds in poisonous tares. Many false doctrines are taught as divine truth. How fearfully God is mistaught! How the divine beauty of His character is marred!

Against all these errors the Christian father must guard his child, and guard him as he would the apple of his eye. These errors have darkened countless souls and have enthroned reason in numberless minds. What fear, dismay, and doubt they have caused in countless thousands of hearts! The snares of vice also lie at every turn of the path, while the whole world is beset with false teachers and deluded with false principles of action.

Against all these the Christian father is to guard

his child; and if he secures him well, his reward and joy in the Christian character and life of his offspring will be great.

4. The father is the natural provider for his child. The child looks to his father to supply his needs as naturally as he looks to him for instruction and protection. The peculiar office of the Christian father is to provide for his children's spiritual needs. Children have spiritual natures which, if provided for in season, will early assume the Christian character and life. We are too apt to undervalue the importance of early Christian training, which is as important to the health and happiness of the mind as early care and training are to the health and happiness of the body.

Among the first things that a Christian father must provide for his children is proper home instruction— lessons in the practical everyday walk of life, which relate to life's duties, blessings, and privileges. These lessons should be drawn from things and events familiar to the child. Stated moral or religious lessons from the Bible or some good book, short and easy to understand, are of great value. Children should also be provided with papers and books adapted to their age and capacity. The Christian father who thus succeeds in faithfully performing his duties to his children sows a harvest of Christian seed that will grow up in honor of Christ both on earth and along the shores of the immortal country.

Study Questions

1. Why does the role of being a father seem a fearful thing?

2. Why cannot a father pass on an inheritance of noble character to his children without first experiencing it himself?

3. How can a Christian father become a perfect father?

4. For what reasons should the father have a strong influence on his children?

5. Discuss what it means to be a true Christian father.

6. Why is it important for the Christian father to have self discipline?

7. What principles make it natural for the Christian father to be his children's most influential teacher?

8. In what ways is the Christian father his children's protector?

9. Why is it of greater importance for parents to provide for their children's spiritual needs than for their physical needs?

Fathers,

Provoke not your children to wrath:
*but bring them up in the nurture
and admonition of the Lord.*

—Ephesians 6:4

Chapter 5

The Christian Mother

We pity anyone who can speak the word *mother* without emotion. To the great mass of humanity no word is as effective as *mother*. It carries them back to the earliest hours of childhood, the days of innocence, when their mother guarded and comforted them, when they went to her with every want and trial and found in her their only changeless friend.[1]

---

[1] It is part of the degeneration of our society today that fewer and fewer children have this sort of relationship with their mother. Many children are raised by baby sitters while their mothers work away. Only eternity will reveal the awful price that such mothers have paid for ignoring their God-given home responsibilities. —EDITOR

They see their mother giving them her time and energies as well as her mind and heart. They see in her the embodiment of maternal affection—one who rejoices in their health and developing powers, who nurses them in sickness, sympathizes with their sorrows, pities them in distress, wipes away their tears, and bids them be happy.

They see her also in her trials, when vice invades her home or disappointment blights her hopes, when she herself is afflicted with sickness, or when doubts and burdens lie upon her soul. And in all these images they see the depth, strength, and beauty of a mother's love. As they look back, they learn both what it is to be a mother, and what great energy of love is needed to bear her up under the burdens and toils of maternity.

We did not understand our mother's soul in childhood or we would have been better children. Had we known our mothers in childhood as we know them now, would we not have lived differently? Would we not have avoided a thousand things we once said and did?

An incident of many years ago might serve to illustrate this point. A woman with several children had been left a widow. The eldest child, a son, necessarily became responsible for a great deal and so had less time to waste than boys with living fathers. Some boys of questionable character took advantage of this eldest son's naturally confiding personality and for a little while succeeded in poisoning his mind against his mother, who, they suggested, was requiring too much from him.

Later he told someone, "One day I saw my mother in a room alone, weeping like a child, after she had been seriously conversing with me about my waywardness and ingratitude, and pointing me to the painful consequences of such a course in life. I knew it was on my account. She thought no one but God saw her. I gazed at her for a few minutes, but the scene was too much for me; my eyes swam with tears; I turned and went away. But I was converted; I saw and felt that I had been shamefully abused by my companions; and my mother became to me again the same person she had been in my younger years. The history of those boys who had led me astray has in every case but one been so bad that I can see no reason why I should not attribute my escape from ruin to the tears my mother shed in a secret place."

So it is. A child cannot comprehend the depth of a mother's love. This mother's tears, accidentally seen, revealed the strength of her love, and that love saved a boy who later became an honored and useful man.

Most of us grow up before we learn what great love was in our mother's heart. Oh, that we could have learned it sooner! It would have saved us from numerous evils. We did not learn profanity from our mothers. Vulgarity came from someone else's lips. Irreverence for religion was taught in a school quite different from hers. A mother's hand did not raise alcohol to our lips, nor did she tell us to put it to our brother's.

A mother's love is pure, sacred, and glorious. With sleepless vigilance it watches the growing child and sees, with a thousand anxieties, that child enter youth. It is not so much a mother's labors, toils, sleepless nights, and unselfish sacrifices that speak so eloquently of her great love, as it is the great anxiety she feels for her children's moral good. How many mothers would rest more peacefully if they knew their children would make good men and women!

It is a holy and a blessed thing to be a mother who is a Christian. The Christian mother possesses all the noble characteristics of the natural mother, but her life and character do not achieve the full dimension that God intended until she is filled with Christian principles. A mother's great influence, together with the intimate and endearing relation she sustains to her children, make it all-important that every mother be a Christian mother.

The duties and obligations of the natural mother are clear; those of a Christian mother will be developed in considering them.

1. The natural mother feeds her children—first from her own breast and later with her hand. But the

Christian mother's obligation goes deeper and higher than this. She must feed their minds and nourish their hearts. She recognizes that her children's minds require as much care and nourishment as their bodies.

The mind grows by a process similar to that of the body. Feed it what you will; it will partake freely of that thing. Hence, its food should be chosen with care and attention. The body will eat and then be satisfied for a season, but not so the mind—its hunger is constant. If not supplied with good food, it will supply itself with anything it can get, good or bad.

Nothing is so greedy as a child's mind. Eyes, ears, hands, and feet are made its servants. The mind, then, should be well fed, and its food of the choicest kind. Everything contains a lesson for the child's mind, from the food he eats and the clothes he wears to the house in which he lives and the people with whom he associates. If a mother is particular about the kind and quality of bodily food she gives her child, she should be even more concerned about his mental and moral food.

Here is just where many mothers are at fault. They spend hours every day feeding their children, but consider it a nuisance to instruct them. But children need such attention almost constantly from their earliest years. If children are well cared for mentally and morally when they are young, they will be little trouble when they are older. As the old proverb says, "Just as the twig is bent, the tree is inclined."

Whether or not she acknowledges it, a mother is a teacher. It is she who begins her child's instruction in the ways of life. She plants the seeds of her child's moral and intellectual life and gives shape and form to his spiritual growth. She does this with words, thoughts, and even looks. If every day she breathes into his receptive spirit lessons of good, beauty, and truth; if every day she taxes his young powers of thought to grasp some new idea of duty or love and tells him something of God and heaven, how surely she will point his gaze heavenward!

Early impressions are strong and very lasting. Mothers should appreciate this fact. They ought to use all their influence and authority to impress upon their children ideas of goodness and religion. Children should be taught to pray as soon as they have any idea of God; to reverence His holy Name and associate it with the idea of a mother's love and care. Let skeptics deny it as they will, the idea of God, deeply impressed upon a young mind, is his best safeguard against evil and his richest inspiration for good.

2. The natural mother clothes her children. They come into the world naked, and so necessity calls her to this duty. Hence all enlightened mothers, like Samuel's mother in the Scriptures, have made "little coats" for their children. The office of the Christian mother corresponds to this. She is to make "little coats" for her children's minds.

Their souls come into the mother's arms as naked as their bodies, and the need for clothing them is as great as that for clothing their bodies. In fact an unclothed soul is infinitely more in need than an unclothed body. If children were left to themselves, they might sew fig leaves together to make themselves aprons, but how little protection such garments would afford them, and to what assaults of wind and weather they would be exposed! Is there anything more tragic than children for whose minds no protection is given?

Every day a mother must weave garments of virtue for her children. Their spirits should be dressed better than their bodies. Outer garments will wear out, but the garments of virtue with which children's spirits are clothed will never wear out. They may rend and soil them, but they can never completely lay them aside or totally destroy them (see Proverbs 22:6).

By clothing her children's spirits a mother is blessed. She thus presents them to both the world and God as beautiful offerings of love and care. When a mother has filled her children with the spirit of filial love and gratitude, they ever cherish her name and memory and "arise up, and call her blessed" (Proverbs 31:28).

3. The natural mother nurses and watches her children when they are sick, and guards them against

disease. The Christian mother's corresponding duty is to nurse and guard her children's minds against disease. Diseases are all about us. Wicked words float on every gale; vicious thoughts, like insects at night, gather around the mind; corrupting examples can be found everywhere; and noxious vapors rise from every stagnant pool in society, fevering the imagination, perverting the affections, and stimulating the wicked ambitions. Who can tell how many such diseases a child is exposed to? Their name is legion. Guarding a child against this pestilence is a mother's most difficult task.

How closely she must watch her children's habits! Every wrong must be nipped in the bud. The first coarse word must receive a reprimand, and the first faint tendency to deception taken in hand. The first sign of selfishness must be plucked up, and seeds of honor and goodness planted in their stead. No evil habit must be allowed to sink its poisonous roots in the young soul of the child.

Teach children early about the evil of evil, the wrong of wrong. They must not be left to discover it by experience. Prejudice them against all sin. Though the word has negative connotations, prejudice is right in its place; so is hate. But both should be turned against wrong.

Nevertheless, even with all this guarding, since the child is carnal by nature, many diseases will creep into his mind. This is why a mother must guide her children in the way of genuine repentance and faith to a place of spiritual regeneration. She must do so patiently, with perseverance and hope. By thus performing her duty, she may experience the blessed privilege of seeing her children grow up to become examples of Christian devotion and usefulness in the world and inhabitants of the Redeemer's kingdom.

Study Questions

1. Why does the word *mother* carry such strong emotions for most people?

2. Why has this pattern changed for many young people in these days?

3. Why is the Christian mother's love so influential in a child's life?

4. What makes it possible for the Christian mother to reach her greatest potential in directing her children toward God?

5. Why is it so important for a child's mind to be filled with good and noble things?

6. What are the results of influencing the child's mind with the existence of God? How can the Christian mother impress her child with the responsibility of serving God without prematurely destroying his God-given innocence?

7. Why will a child do evil even if he has not been taught to do so?

8. What is the mother's responsibility in guarding her children's purity of mind?

Who can find a virtuous woman?

She openeth her mouth with wisdom;
and in her tongue is the law of kindness.

She looketh well to the ways of her household,
and eateth not the bread of idleness.

Her children arise up, and call her blessed;
her husband also, and he praiseth her.

—Proverbs 31:10, 26–28

Chapter 6

Children in the Home

A great event happens when a new baby is born. The parents receive a new creation direct from the hand of God. A baby enters the home in a state of innocence and perfection. Nevertheless, it has the potential for evil that characterizes all mankind. A child comes equipped with a carnal nature that will soon manifest itself to the child's father and mother and that will require constant watchfulness throughout all his childhood.

Childbearing was part of God's created order (see Genesis 1:28), and through it His redemptive plan was fulfilled. Every Jewish mother longed to bear children. Rachel's plea, "Give me children, or else I die" (Genesis 30:1), and Hannah's prayer for a child (see 1 Samuel

1:11) are examples of this desire. One reason for this concern was the possibility that through them the Messiah might come.

There ought to be the same desire for children in our homes, for from godly people will be born men and women who will carry the saving testimony of Christ to the lost world. God's divine plan is that the godly seed shall be salt and light to the whole world.

This call is both a privilege and a responsibility to the Christian home. Children are born with an eternal plan and destiny. They come to us in innocence and remain innocent until by their own choice they reject the mercy of God. In this choice they, like Adam, lose their first innocence.

Thus, raising a child is a great moral mission. The child should be guarded with care and managed with prudence. A sense of judgment and moral rectitude must be impressed upon his heart with steadily increasing force. Nowadays virtues are seldom taught anywhere but in the home, the church, or the Christian school.

Child training brings to the parent lessons that they could not possibly learn otherwise. Its difficulties are great, but its rewards are far greater. It involves subduing our own selfishness. Children provide us with greater incentives to action and virtue than most of our other interests do. They are perhaps our best teachers.

The greatest end of human existence is spiritual

growth. To this end, trial, responsibility, care, and anxiety are as useful as pleasure and joy—often far more so. Children are thus useful in the great economy of parental and family relations. And when this natural relationship is sanctified by Christian faith, it becomes even more glorious.

Even in his early years, a child must be taught that he too has responsibilities. We will consider several of these.

1. A child must learn to honor his father and mother. The child owes his existence to them; from them he received the care and attention necessary to his very life. It is therefore necessary that the child honor his parents in return. To a young child all wisdom, strength, and love reside in his parents. Through the Christian parent a child receives his first concept of God and what God is to man. A kind of reverence springs up in the child, which is later transformed into piety felt towards the Father in heaven.

To honor our parents is not only to *love* but also to *obey* them. God first loved us, and so we should love Him. Similarly, parents first love their child, and the child should love them in return. This is natural. Love begets love. But a good child should obey his parents as well as love them. There can be neither honor nor love without obedience. The disobedient child can become a Christian only when he yields to full and complete obedience.

Love is the supreme Christian principle, and every child that loves others is on the road to becoming a Christian.

2. A child must learn to practice self-denial. Children are apt to be selfish, to wish to supply self at the expense or neglect of others. But where there is true love, there will be self-denial; and where there is self-denial, there can be no angry feelings, no hard words, no ill will. It is selfish to be angry; it is wicked too. In a Christian home, a child must learn to conquer his temper, speak kind words, and do good deeds. Then he will show that love rules his heart.

3. A child must learn the beautiful traits of tenderness and sympathy. All cruelty is wicked. Kindness is the fruit of Christian love. Christ was full of sympathy. All children who aspire to be Christians should be like Christ, neither cruel nor unkind. Cruel children seldom honor their parents. A child must love them to honor them.

4. A child must learn to be honest. Honesty is a vital Christian principle. Most men admire honesty and love honest children. Children who exhibit this virtue are blessings to their parents.

5. Children should learn faith and trust in God from their confidence in their parents. Children who confide in their parents will surely learn to confide in their heavenly Father. He is good and strong and always loves and cares for them. They should think much of His goodness, thank Him often for His care, and love Him always with fervent hearts. It was God who gave them life, who formed their bodies and minds. It is only proper that children should love and trust Him and that they should pray to Him and have faith in Christ, who teaches and has shown by His resurrection that God has prepared for all a life and home beyond the shadow of death.

6. Worship is the most efficient means to impress children's minds with Christian principles. Children learn by small things. They do not grasp a great principle and draw from it deductions that lead into truth. They get as they go, and for them to grow into Christian men and women, they should have as much as possible in the way of Christian influences.

No place is richer in such influences than a Christian home, a Scriptural church and Sunday school, and a Christian school. These three, working together, will do the child much good.

The day soon comes when children are faced with personal decisions. If we have trained them in a Scriptural way, they will have the background of our influence to help them to choose right. Their choices will have eternal consequences. May our parental obligations toward them never allow us to lose our concern for their eternal welfare. Our prayers should constantly arise before our heavenly Father on behalf of the posterity He has so graciously given.

Study Questions

1. How is it that a newborn child is so innocent and perfect, yet has such potential for evil?

2. What are God's reasons for Christian parents to have and train children?

3. What is the greatest goal a parent needs to keep in mind in teaching his children?

4. Why is it so important that a child learn to love, honor, and obey his parents when he is young?

5. Self-denial helps to put into right perspective what natural trait of the carnal nature?

6. Name and discuss the value of other virtues that parents need to teach their children.

Children,

>   **Obey your parents in the Lord:**
>   *for this is right.*
>
>   **Honour thy father and mother . . .**
>
>   **That it may be well with thee,**
>   *and thou mayest live long on the earth.*
>
>   *—Ephesians 6:1–3*

Chapter 7

The Christian Brother

Of all the God-ordained associations formed among men, the family stands first and most important. The family is not simply a sociable association. Men do not form families as birds or sheep form flocks. They do it in answer to a spiritual need and in compliance with divine law.

In the family are formed the domestic relationships, among the first of which is brotherhood. Brotherhood is based on kindredness of blood, nature, and origin. A brother may see himself in his brother if he looks closely. Brothers can learn much about each other by studying themselves.

Brotherhood is one of the eternal facts of spiritual existence. Men and angels both were created by the same heavenly Father, and so a bond of brotherhood unites them. This bond is also mirrored in our families. We grow up with our brothers and sisters as our childhood companions. Hand in hand we mature with them to adulthood, and heart with heart we journey together to grace. If in early life we are properly impressed with this beautiful relationship and grow up with an increasing knowledge of its importance and use, how blessed we are with some of the elements of eternal progress and happiness!

Much depends on starting right in life. If children learn brotherhood—its rights, privileges, and duties—they learn a blessed truth. To be a brother is to inherit a blessed privilege, the privilege of loving and being loved. In brother and sister relations, sorrows are divided and joys are multiplied.

Siblings live mutually. They draw on each other's funds of wisdom and goodness. They tax and retax each other. Thus they sow the seeds of kinship: begin to live and forbear, yield and forgive, persuade and encourage, assist and serve, bless and care for each other.

If the principles of Christian brotherhood can be brought to bear upon the relationship, if young minds can be taught what Jesus Christ has done for them in the world—how He lived and labored for His brothers and sisters in the great family, how He loved and blessed them with His kindly ministrations, how He encouraged the weak, pitied the sick, sorrowed with the disappointed and bereaved, and spoke kindly to the wayward—they will be taught the great lessons of Christian brotherhood.

Natural brotherhood is commendable and beautiful, but Christian brotherhood takes us into the realm of the supernatural. It is natural love sanctified by the living presence of Christ within. The lessons of the Bible should be the daily food of Christian brotherhood.

The life of Christ was the perfect example of Christian brotherhood. Children may be taught to live Christian principles at a young age. Christ's name, reverently spoken, can be a household word as commonly used as *father* or *mother*; the story of His life can be presented daily and understood to be divine. The school should constantly impress Christian lessons to keep strong the idea of Christ's divine origin. Let parents, teachers, and older associates exhibit at all times a deep reverence for Christ, and this will soon develop the habit of making Christ the example to be copied in all things. When a brother so taught comes to know Christ personally, his influence for good will be profound as he relates properly to his brothers and sisters.

Let us now note some of the benefits of such a brother in family life.

1. He is a teacher, not so much by virtue of office as by virtue of his own wisdom and love. His life is an example of wisdom and practical obedience to Christian authority and principle. Being on terms of equality with his brothers and sisters, he is fit to be their teacher in a way that perhaps no one else is.

He may show them how to live. When they err, he may kindly tell them of their wrong, not in the form of a moral lecture or a sermon on duty, but in everyday talk. When a brother tells us we do wrong, it comes to us with a force different from that of other people. His suggestions affect us more lovingly than those of many others who are very near us. A brother is our equal; he understands our feelings, sympathizes with us, and seeks our good.

A brother is often an instructor when no one else can be. But to teach effectively, a brother must be a Christian. When a brother attempts to instruct us fretfully, arrogantly, tauntingly, or in any other way that is not Christian, we are apt to resent it, whereas, if he comes to us in love, we can more easily receive his help, however severe it may be. This is the very point where brothers often fail. Many feel that they have a sort of guaranteed privilege to instruct their brothers and sisters in the language of rebuke, complaint, insult, and anger, and expect their words to be received with perfect docility. Here is where family feuds generally begin.

Some brothers, with good intentions, will make great sacrifices for their brothers and sisters, but they spoil their help with their unchristian manner.

We are not inclined to receive even good instruction from a brother if it is given in an unkind manner. Brotherhood is a noble relationship, but it can be filled only in love.

2. The Christian brother will be a peacemaker. The faultless Prince of Peace said, "Blessed are the peacemakers" (Matthew 5:9). To guard the peace of a family is one of the holiest offices that any of its members may fill. Family relations are so intimate that unless they are closely watched, contentions and disputes could easily arise and destroy the family's moral usefulness. No office of the Christian brother is more noble than that of guarding the family peace.

Contention is out of place in a family, but it does exist. Most families know something of it from bitter experience. A faithful Christian brother in a family will guard peace above all. How does he exercise this office? Generally not by direct influence, but by his own self-control, by calm everyday Christian love, by practicing the principles of the Prince of Peace in everyday life.

3. The Christian brother will assist in and encourage the religious interests of his brothers and sisters. He will instill respect for the Lord's Day, and will faithfully attend church services and seek to make them impressive to his siblings. He will take an active part in family devotions. He will cherish the teachings of the

Bible and seek to make others feel the individual responsibilities of the Christian. He will make the Christian good of his brothers and sisters his own good and will set his Christian character before them in all meekness and humility. He will pray the Father to make his life a blessing to all with whom he associates, and he will remember them in his own devotions.

4. The Christian brother will closely watch the character of those admitted to the household. Knowing that "evil communications corrupt good manners" (1 Corinthians 15:33), he will guard against deceivers. Those who do not themselves possess Christian virtue will find no approval at his hand and no admission to the family confidence. And in this character he will be especially useful to his sisters. They need a Christian brother's confidence and care. To them he can provide an invaluable service. They have less advantage than he to know the real character of those who ask their acquaintance. If he shows concern or doubt, his sisters had better listen.

5. The Christian brother will be a brother through life. True brotherhood will not end when he leaves the paternal roof. It will be a blessing at home and abroad. Separation will neither disturb nor erase it. All along life's crooked way with many checkered scenes, it lives, flourishes, and blesses. And when death is over, it will be manifest in resurrected perfection in the beautiful home above.

Study Questions

1. What are some of the benefits of brotherhood that are experienced in the Christian home?

2. What are the rights, the privileges, and the duties of brotherhood?

3. Christian brotherhood points everyone to Christ. In what ways does it do this?

4. What virtues must a Christian brother put into practice along with the instruction he gives to his siblings?

5. How can a Christian brother exert his influence on behalf of the spiritual interests of his brothers and sisters?

6. Discuss the ways in which a brother can guard the moral and spiritual purity of his sisters in their friendships.

My son,

Hear the instruction of thy father,
and forsake not the law of thy mother.

If sinners entice thee,
consent thou not.

Forget not my law;
*but let thine heart keep my
commandments.*

Despise not the chastening of the LORD;
neither be weary of his correction.

—Proverbs 1:8, 10; 3:1, 11

Chapter 8

The Christian Sister

We have considered several members of the Christian home; now we come to the sister. As many Scriptures show, Christian womanhood holds its own special place in God's plan for the home. The Christian woman is one of the best expressions of Christ's religion that the world affords, and perhaps we can say that the Christian sister is one of the best expressions of Christian womanhood we have among us. The powerful love of the wife and mother is natural and right, but not necessarily Christian. Christian love can be better expressed by the word *charity*. Benevolence, compassion, piety, and affection are the elements of Christian love. The idea of blessing without thought of return, of blessing by example, by influence, by imparting spiritually the affectionate spirit of the Lowly One of Nazareth, is at the bottom of Christian love. Such is the love of the Christian sister who has completely surrendered herself to her Lord and taken her place in the home.

What, then, are the responsibilities of Christian sisters?

1. The Christian sister is to be an example of active love in her household. She is to show the love of her Master, to be the Good Samaritan in her family. She is to make herself a just representative of Him who went about doing good. We always look for large-hearted love in a sister. When that love is Christian, how expansive and unselfish it is! When the sister's anxiety extends to all, when her Christian care and concern breathes prayers for everyone, she exerts a holy influence in her family.

There is still another way the Christian sister may exemplify Christian charity. She will disapprove of uncharitable speech and action at home or elsewhere. If she hears unkind speech, she will gently reprove the speaker. She will always reflect the love of a true Christian, whatever the case.

Families are too frequently hotbeds of common gossip and petty slander. Almost unconsciously, many families acquire the habit of dissecting their neighbors' characters and exposing their supposed faults with relish.

A Christian sister will always put a restraint upon such uncharitable talk at home. Her sisterly affections will instinctively recoil from such conversation, and she will rather seek the good in her neighbors.

2. The Christian sister is to exhibit the beauty of Christian sympathy. Home is sometimes the scene of trial, suffering, and sorrow. Misfortunes, disappointments, accidents, and deaths visit Christian households just as they do others. Situations arise that call for watching, toil, care, patience, and tenderness. Such times as these test the value of Christianity. They express human weakness in language that none can fail to understand, and call for arms stronger than our own. At such times we feel the need for profound Christian sympathy; we wish to feel the beat of another heart to strengthen our own. And who can do this better than a sister who is alive with holy and unselfish love?

No matter what her age, whether beneath the parental roof or in her own house, she needs the strength, love, and beauty of Christian trust and hope to awaken and sanctify her sympathy, both for her brothers and sisters, and for her own household. A sister who bears about her the spirit of Christ and is faithful in bestowing the blessing of her sympathy is truly a Christian sister.

3. The Christian sister is to show the fruits of a pure mind. Affectation, deception, false pretenses, and vanity all repel a pure mind. They grow out of inner corruption. Simplicity of manner and feeling provide good evidence of a pure character. When a sister possesses a pure heart full of Christian love and simplicity, she is a treasure to her brothers and sisters and a blessed presence in her household.

4. The Christian sister is to set an example of active piety. The living flame of devotion should glow deep within her soul.

Such a sister is a blessing of incalculable value to a brother, especially during his youth. She can be an unselfish friend, a safe advisor, a guide, and an inspiration. A brother may confide in her as he could in no one else.

And then, she is still more to him in another respect. She stands as his model woman, the pattern by which he may measure and judge others. And the criterion is a safe one. She affords him a Christian pattern too. This pattern will go with him through life.

A household that has a Christian sister is blest indeed. Her life strikes love-roots into the hearts of all the household, which spring up and grow to the glory of the Lord. God's blessing is on the Christian sister and on the Christian household.

Study Questions

1. How can the virtue of love be expressed by a Christian sister to other members of the family?

2. How can a Christian sister exert a positive influence on the family's speech at home?

3. Discuss how the simple expression of Christian sympathy is a strength rather than a weakness.

4. How does a Christian sister's expressions of a pure mind help her siblings?

5. How does the Christian sister help her brother to establish values as a teenager?

Many daughters have done virtuously,
but thou excellest them all.

Favour is deceitful, and beauty is vain:
but a woman that feareth the LORD,

SHE SHALL BE PRAISED.

—*Proverbs 31:29–30*

Chapter 9

Employment for All

No Christian home is complete unless there is work for every member to do. Household duties should be introduced into the lives of the children at a very early age so that good habits are formed.

Parents are inclined to think that no great responsibility should be given to a child until he is mature mentally and physically. This is a serious mistake, for it is a part of the child's development to learn responsibility.

Activity is part of all our lives. To do and to bear is the duty of life. Study and instruction, careful Scriptural teaching, and good society and environment are all a part of life, but are incomplete unless men, women, and children learn to assume physical responsibilities and work.

Work hardens the muscles, strengthens the body, quickens the blood, sharpens the mind, and corrects the judgment. It makes the child realize that someday he must fill an adult's shoes, bear an adult's part in life, and show himself an adult in doing it.

Nothing will destroy a person's self-respect more quickly than a life of complete idleness. One hundred fifty pounds of bone and muscle do not constitute a man unless he is disciplined to face duties and tasks as a man. A mind full of ideas is not a man unless the governing principle of life directs the ideas to good purpose and fulfillment.

Children should all have a proper attitude toward gainful employment. This is true whether the child is a boy or a girl. Too many girls today lack the true values of womanhood.

A lady and a woman are two different things. One is made by the hand of fashion and careless indulgence; the other is the handiwork of God, partially through useful employment. A pampered lady is a parlor ornament, a walking show gallery, a mistress of etiquette; a true woman in the Biblical sense is a consecrated intelligence, a love baptized in toil and affliction, a hand employed in the work of good. Being a Scriptural woman requires exertion and prudence. Her true virtues blossom in the garden of industrious toil. A woman or man with no employment for the hands can only be a shadow of what God intended her or him to be. What should be noble will soon lose its nobility. What should be strong will become weak, and the person will soon start depending on others.

A dependent life is an ignoble one unless the situation was so ordered by God. A man or woman who wastes a healthy body and mind in a life of idleness cannot fully exercise the careful and explicit teaching of the Word. The physically handicapped sometimes put healthy people to shame in their effort to live useful lives.

All Christian parents should provide good employment for their children to fit them for life. This must be done within a safe, spiritual environment and with wise planning and purpose. Children should be given responsibilities that allow them to make some decisions by themselves. If we make every decision for them, when the day comes that they must make decisions for themselves, they will be unable to make a decision for themselves when the need arises.

A child grows strong by sometimes standing alone. Place an acorn in the crevice of a barren rock, and it will send down its roots until it surrounds the rock with a net of clinging fibers. So it is with man. Place his feet in a hard place where he must stand by his own strength, and he will grow in strength by the very pressure of adverse circumstances.

Every boy and girl should know what it means to

face life when the kind shelter of the home is taken away, or when he or she by God's will leaves it. Far too many enter adult life ill-prepared to face any responsibility. Far too many enter marriage with little or no awareness of what life consists of and of their God-given duties.

The Bible is full of teaching on the value of industry, the folly of neglect, and the responsibility of parents to look well to their households in preparing their children for godly, industrious lives. Some may shirk this responsibility because of a misguided desire to protect their children. But to fail to teach our children the necessity of working and never expose them to duty is cruelty, not affection.

We cannot expect our children to fill the place in life that God intended if we neglect this part of their lives. How can we expect them to have strong character, forceful minds, or worthy thoughts if we fail to exercise them in the strengthening processes of life? When God calls for their personal stewardship of time and talent, how will they answer the call?

No matter how well-to-do the home may be, this principle still carries weight: Idleness ruins body and mind; therefore, whether rich or poor, all must answer God's call to live useful lives, rather than be selfishly employed.

Study Questions

1. Why is learning to work important for a child?

2. What part does work have in the mental and emotional development of a child?

3. In what ways does work teach a child personal responsibility?

4. What Biblical principles about work should we keep in mind when teaching our children to work?

5. How will idleness affect the future attitudes of a child?

For even when we were with you, this we commanded you, that if any would not work, neither should he eat. For we hear that there are some which walk among you disorderly, working not at all, but are busybodies. Now them that are such we command and exhort by our Lord Jesus Christ, that with quietness they work, and eat their own bread.

—2 Thessalonians 3:10–12